Disney · PIXAR

UP

Level 6

Re-told by: Vessela Gasper
Series Editor: Rachel Wilson

Contents

In This Book

Carl Fredricksen

An elderly man, who dreams of adventures

Ellie Fredricksen

Carl's wife, who always wanted to go to Paradise Falls

Russell

A nine-year-old Wilderness Explorer, who needs one more badge

Charles Muntz

A famous explorer, who goes to Paradise Falls

Kevin

A large female bird who lives in Paradise Fallls

Dug

A funny dog, who can speak with the help of a machine

Before You Read

Introduction

Young Carl Fredricksen dreams of adventures and wants to explore South America. He meets Ellie, a little girl with a big dream to visit Paradise Falls. They grow up, become close friends, get married, and build a home together. But they never travel to South America.

After Ellie dies, Carl promises to follow his wife's dream to see Paradise Falls. This is the beginning of an amazing adventure. There are hundreds of balloons, a very large bird, and a talking dog. But Carl discovers that the biggest adventure is meeting a boy named Russell …

Activities

1 **Use the *Glossary* to find the meaning of these words. On which page do you first see them?**

1 goggles   **3** rope   **5** helmet   **7** hose

2 badge   **4** net   **6** porch   **8** skeleton

2 **Look at the pictures and answer the questions.**

1 (page 13) Why are balloons important in the story?

2 (page 14) Where is Russell? How does he feel? Why?

3 (page 16) Where are they? What's happening?

4 (page 19) Who is the boy giving food to? Why is he doing that?

1 Young Carl Meets Ellie

Young Carl Fredricksen dreamed of adventures. He often wore goggles and a helmet because he imagined he was an explorer. One day, he was watching a news film about the famous explorer Charles Muntz.

In the film, Muntz returned in his airship from Paradise Falls in South America. A crowd was waiting. Everyone wanted to see what he had. Muntz proudly showed them the skeleton of a *very* tall bird!

But after scientists looked at it, they were unhappy. They said the skeleton was not real. Muntz promised to return and bring the bird back alive. There, the news film ended.

Afterward, Carl imagined his blue balloon was his airship and he was flying home. His balloon floated over his head. Suddenly, he heard a loud voice coming from an old house, "Adventure is out there!"

He walked up the steps and on to the porch. He listened, then went inside. Upstairs, Carl found a girl at an open window. She was wearing goggles and a helmet and she was steering her "ship." Carl noticed photos on the wall of his favorite explorer—Charles Muntz. Suddenly, the girl turned and saw Carl.

"This is a clubhouse!" the girl shouted. Surprised, Carl let his balloon float away. Carl noticed her badges, which she made from the tops of used bottles. She took off a badge and put it on Carl.

She smiled and said, "You and me—we're in a club now. I saw where your balloon went. Let's go get it!" she said. "My name's Ellie."

Carl's balloon was near a hole in the roof. Slowly, he walked toward his balloon ... then ... *CRASH!* Oh, no! Carl fell through the floor and broke his arm!

That evening, Carl was in bed with his broken arm when Ellie climbed in through the open window.

"I've got something to show you," she said. "You have to promise you won't tell anyone." Carl agreed. "Cross your heart!" she said. Carl crossed his heart.

Ellie showed him a book with the words *My Adventure Book* on the front. Inside, Carl saw a picture of Muntz and a map of South America. On a picture of Paradise Falls was Ellie's picture of her clubhouse. Ellie planned to put her clubhouse at the top of Paradise Falls.

When Ellie turned the page, Carl saw blank pages ready for new pictures and adventures. "I'm saving these pages for all the adventures I'm going to have," she continued. "Only, I just don't know how I'm going to get to Paradise Falls."

She thought for a minute. Suddenly, she had an idea! Carl could take them both there, she told him. "Cross your heart!" she ordered. Carl quickly crossed his heart.

"See you tomorrow!" said Ellie happily. She picked up her book and climbed out of the window. From the window, Carl's eyes followed this beautiful, amazing girl.

"Wow," he said.

2 Happy Dreams

Carl and Ellie became best friends. Years later, they married and bought Ellie's old clubhouse. They fixed the floors and windows, and painted the whole house. Ellie put two comfortable chairs in front of the window so they could sit together every evening. She painted their names on the mailbox, too.

They both got jobs at the zoo. Carl sold balloons at the zoo gates and Ellie looked after the animals there. They happily dreamed about their future.

Carl and Ellie enjoyed their jobs at the zoo but they still dreamed of Paradise Falls. Maybe they couldn't be explorers, but they could still travel to South America.

Carl put a large bottle on a table and they put money into it as often as possible. They were saving for their adventure to Paradise Falls.

But every time the bottle got half full, something happened. They had to fix the car and pay for a new roof. Then, Carl broke his leg and they had to pay the hospital. They could never fill that bottle with coins.

Many years passed. Carl realized they were getting old and decided to buy tickets to Venezuela. He wanted Ellie to visit Paradise Falls before it was too late. But before they could leave, she got sick. Carl took her to the hospital. Then, Ellie sadly died.

After that, Carl sat in his armchair, sad and alone. He looked at her empty chair and thought about his wonderful wife. He remembered all their dreams.

3 On Their Way

Year after year, Carl's house stayed the same. He missed Ellie very much and kept everything the way she liked it.

But things were not the same. His neighborhood was changing. Builders were building offices around his house. Carl was very unhappy. Now, when he walked out of his front door, he saw engineers and machines. It was also very noisy.

Carl's neighbors sold their houses, but Carl didn't want to sell his home. The house meant too much to him.

One day, someone knocked on Carl's door. A boy in a Wilderness Explorers uniform was standing on the porch. He said his name was Russell. He needed to get his Wilderness Explorer's badge for helping the elderly.

Carl didn't want help. He wanted the boy to leave. So Carl told Russell that a bird was eating his flowers. This wasn't true, of course, but Russell ran to look for it. "Bring it back here when you find it!" Carl shouted.

Later that day, the builder's truck accidently hit Carl's mailbox. Carl angrily hit the builder with his walking stick. That wasn't sensible. A police officer came. Carl was in trouble.

After that, Carl had to move to a home for the elderly. The night before the move, he opened Ellie's *My Adventure Book*. He looked at the picture of her clubhouse at Paradise Falls. He sadly closed the book.

Carl remembered his promise to Ellie. He crossed his heart. Then Carl had an idea. Maybe it wasn't too late ... and maybe Ellie could go, too.

The next morning, two men in green uniforms came to take Carl to the home for the elderly. Carl gave them his suitcase. He went back inside because he wanted to say one last goodbye to his old house.

The men were walking back to their car with Carl's suitcase when they heard a loud noise. They turned and saw something amazing!

Thousands of balloons on ropes were coming out of the roof! They were pulling the house UP off the ground and high UP into the air! The garden hose went with the house UP into the sky!

Carl looked out the window at the two men and laughed. The house floated above their heads and over buildings. Now he was a real explorer on a real adventure.

He tied blankets to ropes outside the windows so his house could sail across the sky. He was steering his floating house with more ropes.

A map of South America was on the table next to Ellie's old picture of Paradise Falls. Carl looked at the photo of Ellie on the wall. He said softly, "We're on our way, Ellie!"

4 Russell Knocks on the Door

Carl was smiling when he sat down and closed his eyes.

KNOCK! KNOCK! KNOCK! Suddenly, a sound surprised him. Carl got up and opened the door. At first, he didn't see anyone. He only saw clouds. Then, he turned his head … and jumped!

"Hello, Mr. Fredricksen. It's me. Russell." Russell was on the porch, holding on to the house.

"What are you doing out here, boy?"

"I followed the bird under the porch. But the bird had a long tail … and it looked … more like a mouse. Please let me in," Russell said nervously.

Inside, Russell picked up Ellie's picture of Paradise Falls. "Are you going to South America, Mr. Fredricksen?"

"Don't touch that!" Carl shouted.

Suddenly, the sky became dark. It began to rain and they were immediately in a terrible storm. Carl tried to steer the house away from the storm, but it was impossible. The house moved from side to side and the furniture fell over. Something hit Carl's head and he fell on the floor. When Carl's eyes opened, he spoke. "Where are we?" He got up and looked out the window.

"I steered us to South America," said Russell proudly.

Carl cut some ropes and the house began to float down to the land below. Carl and Russell stood on the porch together. "We're high up. It could take hours to get down," Carl told Russell.

Suddenly, the house passed a very tall rock. And then another tall rock! "We can't be close to the ground yet!" shouted Carl nervously. Then, the house hit a rock. Carl and Russell fell off the porch. The garden hose came down and Carl grabbed it. Russell grabbed Mr. Fredricksen's leg.

Suddenly, the house was going UP! It was pulling them through the air!

Shortly after, the house floated down, so Russell's feet were on a rock. He pulled hard on Carl's legs. Then, they were both standing on the rock with the house above them.

There was a thick fog so it was difficult to see anything. But, slowly the fog disappeared and the sky was clear again. Carl's eyes opened wide. Not very far away, he saw … Paradise Falls! The water was falling from a great height and it looked exactly the same as Ellie's picture.

Carl looked around at the rocks and jungle below. "Ellie," said Carl quietly, "it's so beautiful!"

5 Following the Tracks

Russell was thinking about his badge for helping the elderly, so he offered to help Mr. Fredricksen. Together, they could pull the house across the rocky land to Paradise Falls. Carl agreed.

But after they walked for an hour, Russell's legs were tired. Soon after that, he needed to go to the toilet. Russell left Mr. Fredricksen and went into the thick jungle near a group of trees.

Suddenly, he noticed some tracks. He was excited. They were large tracks from a very large bird! They were from the bird who ate Mr. Fredricksen's flowers! Russell was sure!

Russell followed the tracks until they disappeared near some large plants. He stopped and looked around. Then, he took a bar of chocolate out of his pocket and bit into it.

Suddenly, a bird bit off a piece of Russell's chocolate bar. Russell got down on his knees and looked under the leaves. He offered the bird more chocolate. The bird bit off another piece.

"Hi, boy. Don't eat it all. Come on out," Russell said softly. As the bird came out, Russell looked up. It was thirteen feet tall! The colorful bird followed Russell back to Mr. Fredricksen.

When Russell returned with the bird, Carl screamed. He grabbed
Russell, but then the bird grabbed Russell, too. The bird wanted to
play. It threw Russell into the air and caught him. Russell laughed.
Carl tried to send the bird away. When the bird tried to attack Carl,
Russell stopped it.

"It's okay, Kevin, Mr. Fredricksen is nice," Russell said.

"Kevin?" asked Carl.

"Yes, that's the name I just gave him. Can I keep him?"

"No," said Carl. Carl and Russell continued toward Paradise
Falls. Russell dropped pieces of chocolate on the ground and so
Kevin followed, too.

Suddenly, they heard a voice. Kevin ran away. "I can smell you," the voice said. A friendly dog joined them.

When Russell said, "Sit!" the dog sat. When Russell said, "Speak!" the dog said, "My name is Dug." Dug explained about the machine around his neck. With it, he could speak. He told them he was tracking a bird.

Suddenly, Kevin returned and jumped on Dug. Dug was very excited. "May I take your bird as my prisoner?" asked Dug.

"Yes!" said Carl.

Dug said to Kevin, "Please be my prisoner … please!" So Dug followed Kevin, Russell, and Carl to Paradise Falls.

That night, Russell tried building a tent, but it was impossible. His dad was going to show him, but he didn't see him often, he told Mr. Fredricksen. But Russell's dad *was* planning to go to the next Wilderness Explorers ceremony. He wanted to see Russell receive his badge for helping the elderly, Russell explained.

Russell was silent for some minutes. Then he spoke. "Mr. Fredricksen, Dug says he wants Kevin for his prisoner. We have to look after Kevin. Can he come with us?"

"Yes," said Carl.

"Cross your heart?" Russell asked Carl. These were Ellie's words.

Carl thought for a minute. Then he replied, "Cross my heart."

6 Kevin Is in Trouble

The next morning, Russell discovered that Kevin was a female! He found her on the roof of the house. "The bird is calling to her babies," explained Dug.

Kevin heard their cries and quickly went to find them. Russell wanted to go with her, but Carl didn't let him. He wanted to get to the Falls as quickly as possible. "She can take care of herself," he told Russell.

Just after Kevin left, three fierce dogs arrived. They knew Dug and they were looking for the bird. They were angry that she was gone. The three dogs led Carl and Russell to a cave. Soon, hundreds of other fierce dogs joined them! Carl and Russell were frightened.

Suddenly, they heard a man's voice. "You came here in *that*?" the man asked. He pointed at Carl's house and laughed.

"Well, I'm not an engineer …," Carl started saying. Then his eyes opened wide. "Are you Charles Muntz?" he cried. Muntz invited Carl and Russell into his airship for supper.

Carl was excited when Muntz took him through his museum full of skeletons. They enjoyed their supper and conversation. But when Muntz walked over to a skeleton of a very tall bird, he began to change. He spoke about his whole life's work on one job—tracking that bird!

"That looks like Kevin!" said Russell.

"Kevin?" Muntz asked. Russell explained about Kevin.

Carl began to worry. "But it ran away!" he said nervously.

Suddenly, they heard a loud cry. Muntz looked out and saw Kevin on Carl's house. He wanted that bird! Carl grabbed Russell. They had to save Kevin!

"Get them!" Muntz shouted to his dogs. Fierce dogs ran after Carl and Russell. Dug saw that they were in trouble.

"Over here!" Dug shouted to Carl.

Carl and Russell grabbed the hose and rope and ran away with the house. The dogs were getting closer. Kevin jumped down from the roof and grabbed Carl and Russell. She put them on her back and ran.

When Dug tried to stop the dogs, one of them threw him off a tall rock. But Dug didn't fall very far. Kevin jumped over more and more high rocks.

Kevin was running as fast as she could. "Give me your hand!" Carl shouted. Russell grabbed Carl's hand and Carl grabbed Dug.

Suddenly, Kevin stopped. She looked down at the river very far below. The dogs were coming faster and faster! She jumped. When the dogs tried to jump, a lot of them fell down into the river.

Kevin got Carl and his friends safely across, but she hurt her leg. Carl looked down at the dogs, who were swimming in the river. The dogs on the other side turned and ran. Russell looked after Kevin's leg.

Suddenly, Kevin heard her babies' cries. She tried to stand but fell down. Russell was worrying about Kevin's leg. He wanted to help her to go home. Carl wanted to continue to Paradise Falls, but he had to help Kevin. He was grateful to her.

They put Kevin on the porch of the floating house. Then they started walking to Kevin's home. They almost reached her babies when suddenly a bright light shone down on Kevin. Russell shouted, "Run, Kevin!" A large net came down over Kevin and she fell to the ground.

Russell and Carl ran to Kevin. Carl took out his knife and started cutting the net. "Get away from my bird!" shouted Muntz.

Then Muntz threw his burning torch on Carl's porch. Carl couldn't believe what he saw. His house was burning! Quickly, he grabbed a blanket and started putting out the fire. Muntz's dogs grabbed Kevin and ran back into the airship. Muntz had Kevin now.

"Kevin!" screamed Russell. He was angry with Mr. Fredricksen. "You gave away Kevin!" Carl was angry, too. He grabbed the hose and walked all night. Russell and Dug sadly followed.

7 Carl Fights Back

In the morning, Carl and Russell arrived at Paradise Falls. At last, Ellie's clubhouse was exactly where it was in Ellie's drawing.

Inside the house, Carl picked up Ellie's *My Adventure Book*. He sadly looked at the pages full of Ellie's dreams of adventure. Then, on one page he read, *Things I'm going to do*. He thought that these pages were empty, but no!

For the first time, Carl saw Ellie's photos. There were a lot of photos of their happy years together! And a note from Ellie— *Thanks for the adventure! Now, go have a new one!*

Carl smiled and went out to look for Russell. "I'm going to help Kevin!" Russell shouted angrily from the roof. He was tying some balloons to his back, which carried him UP ... and away!

"No, Russell, no!" shouted Carl. Carl had to help Russell. But there weren't enough balloons now and the house was too heavy. Carl threw all of his furniture out of the house. The house started floating UP! Carl steered the house toward Muntz's airship with Dug beside him.

Russell's balloons took him to Muntz's airship. He jumped inside. But the dogs found Russell and tied him to a chair with a rope. Muntz saw Carl's house floating toward him. "Guard that bird!" he told one of his dogs.

Suddenly, a door flew open and Russell's chair moved out toward the big blue sky! Carl saw this. He rescued Russell and carried him inside his house. Then, Carl and Dug jumped into the airship and found Kevin. But Muntz found them! He attacked Carl! Carl fought back!

When Russell tried to untie the rope around his chair, he fell off the porch! He quickly grabbed the hose. Muntz saw Russell and sent his pilot dogs in planes to attack him. But Russell climbed up the hose and into the house. Carl, Kevin, and Dug climbed to the roof of the airship. Muntz followed them. Russell steered the house toward his friends. They jumped into the house but Carl fell out, onto the roof of the airship.

Suddenly, Muntz broke open the door of the house. Carl shouted, "Russell! Hold on to Kevin! Kevin! Here's some chocolate!" Kevin ran out of the door with Russell and Dug. When Muntz tried to grab them, his foot caught some balloons and he floated away. "Ahhh!" he screamed.

Carl was holding the hose and pulling it hard. Suddenly, the hose broke away from the house. Carl looked over the side of the airship. What good luck! Russell, Kevin, and Dug were holding the other end of the hose! Carl laughed as he pulled them up. He was very happy to see his friends alive!

But suddenly, he saw his house—floating away! Russell said sadly, "I'm sorry about your house, Mr. Fredricksen."

Carl put his arm around Russell's shoulder. "It's just a house," said Carl. He didn't need his house now because he had good friends.

They took Kevin back to her babies in Muntz's airship. Kevin's babies were happy to see their mommy. Dug cheered as Carl and Russell played with the baby birds. Soon it was time for Kevin and her family to go deep into the jungle for the night.

"Bye, Kevin!" Russell called as they walked away. Kevin turned and looked at her friends. They waved goodbye.

Soon, Carl and Russell were steering the airship back home together. They were wearing their goggles and helmets. Russell was happy because he was helping Mr. Fredricksen.

8 Russell Gets the Badge

Back home, Russell arrived for the Wilderness Explorers ceremony. The leader was giving badges for proud fathers to put on their sons. But Russell's father was missing.

"Russell, is there someone …?" asked the leader.

"I'm here for him," said a voice. The leader gave Russell's badge to Mr. Fredricksen. But when Russell looked down at his badge, it wasn't the right one! "It's the Ellie badge," said Carl. It was the old top from a bottle.

"Wow!" said Russell happily. Carl smiled. He knew there were more adventures to come for him and his new friends.

After You Read

1 In the story, who does these things and why? Who ...

1 goes to Paradise Falls in an airship?

2 keeps a secret book?

3 crosses their heart?

4 buys a clubhouse?

5 helps Mr. Fredricksen?

2 Read and Say True or False.

1 Ellie goes to Paradise Falls.

2 Carl does not want to live in a home for the elderly.

3 Carl has a bird that eats his flowers.

4 Russell wants to go to Paradise Falls.

5 Russell steers the house to South America.

3 Who says this? Who do they say it to?

1 "You have to promise you won't tell anyone."

2 "May I take your bird as my prisoner?"

3 "Get away from my bird!"

4 "You gave away Kevin!"

5 "Hold on to Kevin! Kevin! Here's some chocolate!"

Glossary

adventure (*noun*) something you do which is exciting and different, possibly dangerous

badge (*noun*) a small piece of metal or plastic that you wear to show something you have done, or to show that you belong to a group

ceremony (*noun*) an important meeting where a person receives something for a good, or important, thing they have done

cross your heart (*idiom*) you say this when you ask someone to promise they will do something

disappear past tense **disappeared** (*verb*) if something disappears, you can't see it; the opposite of appear; *Russell followed the tracks until they disappeared near some large plants.*

the elderly (*noun*) people who are old

explorer (*noun*) a person who travels to places where not many people have visited before

float past tense **floated** (*verb*) to stay in the air, or move slowly through the air; *His balloon floated over his head.*

goggles (*noun*) close-fitting glasses that keep your eyes safe, for example, when you go swimming

grab past tense **grabbed** (*verb*) to suddenly take someone or something with your hand; *Russell grabbed Carl's hand and Carl grabbed Dug.*

helmet (*noun*) a hard hat that covers your head

hose (*noun*) something that is long, and made of plastic, and can carry water from one place to another

net (*noun*) something you use for catching things

porch (*noun*) a part of a house at the front or back, with a floor and roof, but no walls

prisoner (*noun*) someone who is in prison for doing bad or wrong things

rope (*noun*) something that is strong, thick, and made of many long strings

safely (*adv*) to do something in a way that is not dangerous

skeleton (*noun*) all the hard parts in the body of a person or an animal

tie past tense **tied** (*verb*) to hold two or more things together using a rope; *But the dogs found Russell and tied him to a chair with a rope.*

track (*noun*) the shape or line that a person, an animal or a moving thing, leaves on the ground

Play: Protect Wildlife

Scene 1:

Carl and Russell are having dinner with Muntz inside his airship. He is showing them a skeleton of a large bird.

MUNTZ: [proudly showing the skeleton] This is my life and work! I must find this bird.

RUSSELL: Hey, that looks like Kevin!

MUNTZ: [angrily] Kevin?!

CARL: [quietly to Russell] Err, I think we're in trouble!

Suddenly they hear Kevin outside. She has followed Russell to the airship.

KEVIN: [offstage] Caw, caw, caw!

CARL: Oh, no! That's Kevin! Run!

MUNTZ: [to his guard dogs] Get them!

Scene 2:

Carl and Russell are pulling the house in the jungle. Kevin is hurt and lying on the porch.

RUSSELL: Muntz is looking for Kevin. He'll lock her up.

Suddenly, a large net falls on Kevin. Muntz and his dogs arrive.

RUSSELL: [looking around] What's happening?

CARL: Russell, give me your knife! [he tries to cut the net]

MUNTZ: [walking toward them] Get away from my bird!

Muntz's dogs pull Kevin away.

RUSSELL: [cries] Let her go!

Scene 3:

Carl is inside the airship. Kevin is in a cage. The dogs are guarding the cage.

CARL: It's time to save Kevin. Here, dogs—catch! [he throws a ball]

The dogs run after the ball. Carl gets Kevin.

Scene 4:

Back in the jungle. Kevin is back with her babies. Carl and Russell are happy.

RUSSELL: Kevin is safe now.

CARL: And her babies are, too!

Global Citizenship

Save the Kiwi

The World Wildlife Fund, or WWF, works to protect animals around the world. In New Zealand, the WWF is helping the kiwi from becoming extinct.

Kiwi are small, land birds that only live in New Zealand. Most things about them are different than other birds. They don't fly—they live on the forest floor. Their strong, heavy legs are perfect for life on the ground. They are awake at night and they use their good sense of smell and touch to find food in the dark.

Kiwi are endangered. Before people arrived in New Zealand, there were millions of them. Now there are only about 70,000 left in the wild. The WWF is teaching people how to protect the kiwi.

The kiwi egg is very large. It's about 20 percent the size of the mother's body.

Find Out

Which are the world's most amazing waterfalls?

Angel Falls in Venezuela is the world's highest waterfall. It is 979 meters high. In the summer heat, the water turns to mist before it reaches the bottom.

The idea for Paradise Falls in the story **UP** comes from Angel Falls.

Victoria Falls is a waterfall in southern Africa, between Zambia and Zimbabwe. It is 1,708 meters wide and 108 meters high. It is the largest waterfall in the world.

It is one of the Seven Natural Wonders of the world. It is also a very powerful waterfall. You can hear it from 40 kilometers away.

Niagara Falls is the name of a group of three waterfalls between Canada and the United States. It is about 50 meters high.

It is the most popular waterfall in the world. Around 30 million people go to see Niagara Falls every year. Boats can take people very close to the falls. Watching the falling water in the mist is amazing.

Iguazu Falls is the largest group of waterfalls in the world. There are 275 falls, 2.7 kilometers wide.

The falls are between Argentina and Brazil. Most of them are about 64 meters high. Iguazu Falls is a UNESCO World Heritage Site. The word *iguazu* means *big water.*

million (*number*) 1,000,000
powerful (*adj.*) strong; with a lot of power

43

Phonics

Say the sounds. Read the words.

ear

clear

year

eer

cheer

steer

Read, then say the rhyme to a friend.

Oh dear, oh dear, look at the engineer,
And his big airship that he can't even steer!

Oh dear, oh dear, it's very clear,
This engineer will never disappear!

Oh dear, oh dear, it's another New Year,
Let's give a cheer for the engineer.